Wolf Hill

Toxic Waste

Roderick Hunt

Illustrated by Alex Brychta

OXFORD
UNIVERSITY PRESS

OXFORD
UNIVERSITY PRESS

Great Clarendon Street, Oxford, OX2 6DP

Oxford   New York
Athens   Auckland   Bangkok   Bogotá   Buenos Aires   Calcutta
Cape Town   Chennai   Dar es Salaam   Delhi   Florence   Hong Kong
Istanbul   Karachi   Kuala Lumpur   Madrid   Melbourne   Mexico City
Mumbai   Nairobi   Paris   São Paulo   Singapore   Taipei   Tokyo
Toronto   Warsaw

and associated companies in
Berlin   Ibadan

Oxford is a trade mark of Oxford University Press

© text Roderick Hunt 1998
© illustrations Alex Brychta 1998
First Published 1998
Reprinted 1999

ISBN 019 918660 X

Printed in Hong Kong

2

Chapter 1

Andy was unhappy. Why? It was because of Jools.

'This is Jools,' Andy's mum said. Jools had long hair. It was tied back in a pony tail.

Jools wore glasses with sun shades clipped to them. The shades were on hinges. They stood up flat against his forehead. They made him look like an insect.

'Hi!' said Jools.

'How would you feel if Jools came to stay with us for a few days?' asked Andy's mum.

Andy felt sick. He didn't want a man staying with them. He liked things as they were - just him and his mum.

'He can't stay,' said Andy.

'Why not?' said Andy's mum.

'I don't want him staying here. I hate him,' Andy shouted. He ran outside.

'Andy! Come back,' shouted his mum.

Chapter 2

Kat went round to play with Loz.
Loz was at her Gran's house.

'Shall we play in the den?' asked
Kat.

'OK,' said Loz. 'I'll just tell Gran
first.'

The den was an air-raid shelter. It
was like a little room underground.
It had brick steps going down to it.
Loz had found it by accident.

Loz stopped on the steps of the den.

'There's someone down there,' she said.

'Who's there?' called Kat.

It was Andy. He had been crying.
'I've been here all afternoon,' he said. 'Sorry, Loz. I don't want to go home.'

Chapter 3

Andy told Kat and Loz about Jools. 'I don't like him,' said Andy, 'and Mum wants him to stay with us.'

Just then, someone came down the steps of the den.

'Can I come in?' said a voice.

It was Jools. Andy's Mum was with him.

'What does he want?' hissed Andy.

Jools peered in. 'This is a great den,' he said.

Nobody answered.

'I'm sorry, Andy,' said Jools. 'We don't want to upset you.'

Andy said nothing

'Listen,' said Andy's mum. 'Jools wants to take us fishing. Tomorrow morning, early start. How about it?'

'Lucky you,' said Kat. Loz grinned.

'You could bring your friends,' went on Jools.

Andy thought for a moment.

'OK,' he said.

Chapter 4

The next day they set off in Andy's mum's old car. It was still dark.

Andy kept yawning. Kat wanted to go back to sleep.

'I've never been awake this early,' said Loz.

'It's the best time to go fishing,' said Jools.

Jools knew a good place to fish. It took half an hour to drive there.

'Stop here,' said Jools. 'The river's not far.'

They had to walk across a field. Andy's mum brought a picnic so there was a lot to carry.

They sat down by some trees.
'We'll start fishing when it gets
lighter,' Jools said.

But they didn't. Something
happened. It made them forget
about going fishing.

Chapter 5

Loz and Kat lay on the rug. Andy's mum sat with them. Kat curled up. She wanted to go to sleep again.

Jools had forgotten his fishing bait.
He and Andy went back to the car
and got it.

Suddenly, they heard the sound of
an engine. It came from the other
side of the river. Lights swept across
the field. A big truck backed up to
the edge of the water.

'They're up to something,' hissed Jools. 'Keep down!'

He bent low and ran back to the others. Andy followed.

'Lie flat,' hissed Jools. 'Don't let them see you.'

'What are they doing?' asked Andy.

Chapter 6

The truck was a tanker. Andy could see the word 'toxic' on the back.

Two men were on the bank. They had a long, wide hose. One of the men put the hose in the river.

'Oh no!' said Jools. 'They're going to wash the tanker out. They're going to wash chemicals into the river.'

'But that will poison the river,' said Andy. 'It will kill the fish.'

'I know,' said Jools. 'We've got to stop them. We haven't got much time.'

'Why not just shout at them?' said Loz. 'Maybe that will scare them off.'

'No,' said Jools. 'We've got to stop them for good.'

He started to rub dirt on his face and hands.

'I need your help,' he said.

Chapter 7

On the other bank, the men were
nervous. They worked quickly. They
wanted to get away.

One of the men heard a noise. It
came from the river. 'Plop! Plop!' it
went.

'What was that?' he said.

'Plop! Plop!' went the noise again. It came from lower down the river.

The men looked at the water. They looked along the bank. 'Plop! Plop!' went the noise.

The men walked towards the
noise. Something hit the water.
'Splash!' it went.

Suddenly an engine roared into
life. It was the tanker. There was a
grinding of gears.

24

The tanker started to move. Then it roared across the field.

The men ran after it. 'Stop!' they shouted.

Loz, Andy and Kat stopped
throwing stones into the river.

'Time to go,' said Andy's mum.
'Get back to the car. Leave
everything. Just run for it.'

Chapter 8

Andy's mum drove home.
Everyone was excited. But they felt
frightened, too.

'I hope Jools will be all right,' said
Kat.

'Where has he gone?' asked Loz.

'He went to the police,' said
Andy's mum.

'The way he drove that tanker,'
said Andy. 'It was brilliant!'

They went back to Andy's flat.
Andy's mum made them some
breakfast.

Then the phone rang. It was the
police. Andy's mum spoke to them.
Then she put the phone down.

'We have to go to the police
station,' she said. 'They want to
know why Jools took the tanker.'

'Do they think he stole it?' gasped Kat.

'I suppose he did, in a way,' said Andy's mum. 'That's why they want to see us. We have to tell them what really happened.'

Chapter 9

Andy, Kat and Loz felt famous. There was a picture of them in the newspaper.

'Look,' said Loz. 'It says "Kids in pollution drama".'

She read on. 'It says "Children helped save the River Axe from pollution. The children from Wolf Hill School . . .".'

Najma threw a ball at Loz. It hit the newspaper with a smack.

'Hey!' said Loz. 'Why did you do that?'

'You've read it out four times already,' said Gizmo.

Just then, someone came down the steps of the den.

'Can I come in?' said a voice.

It was Jools.

'I've come to say goodbye,' said Jools.

'You're not staying with us, then?' said Andy.

'No, not just yet,' said Jools.

'But we never did go fishing,' said Andy.

'We'll try again soon,' said Jools. 'Next time we might even catch a fish!'